The Amazing Mr Mulch

Rosemary Hayes

Illustrated by Ian Newsham

CAMBRIDGE
UNIVERSITY PRESS

The bell went for the beginning of school and everyone in
Class 8 ran inside. It was the first day of term and their
new teacher had arrived. He was called Mr Mulch.

"Has anyone seen him?" asked Sarah.

"I saw him in the staffroom," said Craig. "He was sitting in a corner all by himself."

The rest of Class 8 crowded round Craig.

"What did he look like?"

"Is he old?"

"Is he fat?"

"Is he thin?"

"Is he bald?"

Craig frowned and chewed his lip. "Well . . ." he began.

At that moment, Mr Mulch shuffled into the classroom. He looked very confused. He was wearing an old pair of trousers and a jacket which was far too small for him. He stood in front of Class 8 and blinked. His spectacles had slipped to the end of his nose and he pushed them back into place.

"Er . . . Class 8?" he asked. His voice was a bit wobbly.

"No," said someone. "This is Class 9." The rest of the class giggled.

Mr Mulch looked even more confused. "Oh. Oh dear," he said.

Sarah felt sorry for him. "It's all right, Mr Mulch," she said. "This is Class 8. You *are* in the right place."

"Oh. Oh good," said Mr Mulch, looking relieved. He hitched up his trousers and perched on the edge of the nearest table.

"Er . . . perhaps I'd better learn your names," he began. He sounded very nervous.

Class 8 exchanged glances. This was going to be fun!

"My name's Sam," said Oliver.

"My name's Gemma," said Sima.

"My name's Matthew," said Farhan.

"My name's Bonnie," said Claire.

Mr Mulch frowned and blinked his eyes behind his
spectacles. "Sam, Gemma, Matthew, Bonnie," he muttered.
Everyone laughed, except Sarah.

Mr Mulch looked flustered. He picked up some books and handed them out.

"We did this last term!" shouted Claire.

"Yeah! We've done all this," said Oliver.

Mr Mulch stared helplessly at the children. "Oh. Oh dear," he said, "but I was told . . ." Mr Mulch looked as though he was going to bolt out of the door like a frightened rabbit.

Craig stood up. "Don't take any notice of them, Mr Mulch," he said. "We haven't done it. They're just messing about."

Mr Mulch looked gratefully at Craig. "Oh . . . er . . . right. In that case, please turn to page five."

He stood up and clutched at his trousers. "Quiet, please," he said.

But his voice was so soft that Class 8 took no notice of him and went on talking.

When the bell went for break, Mr Mulch sat with his eyes closed and his hands over his ears while Class 8 swarmed about him like noisy bees. Oliver, Sima, Claire and Farhan were the noisiest of all.

At break time, everyone was outside. Mr Mulch wandered around the playground muttering to himself, his hands clasped behind his back. Craig and Sarah felt sorry for him. They went up to him.

"Where do you come from, Mr Mulch?" asked Sarah.

Mr Mulch looked startled. "Er . . . What?"

"Do you live in town?" asked Craig.

Mr Mulch stared over their heads. "No," he said slowly. "No. Where I come from, we are all magicians."

"Magicians!" said Sarah. "You mean everyone is a magician?"

Mr Mulch nodded sadly. "Everyone," he said. Then suddenly he smiled and his whole face lit up. "That's it!" he shouted happily. "I've got it. I know what I'll teach you!" Mr Mulch rubbed his hands together, then he bounded away.

The children looked at each other.

"I like him," said Sarah, "but I think he's nuts."

"Completely nuts," agreed Craig.

After break, Mr Mulch was a changed man. He bounced into the classroom and clapped his hands.

"A pencil!" he roared. "Someone give me a pencil!"

He took a pencil, stared at it, turned it round in his hands and muttered a few words. Class 8 watched with open mouths as, very slowly, the pencil began to grow. It grew to the size of a cucumber. Then it grew even bigger.

Suddenly, Mr Mulch let go of the huge pencil and it burst into life. Everyone ducked as it roared round the classroom like a rocket. Then it shot through the window and out over the town.

Class 8 were amazed.

"Do more!" shouted Farhan. "What else can you do?"

Mr Mulch rubbed his hands together. "Oh, that's nothing," he said modestly.

A moment later, Oliver noticed Farhan's hair.

"Your hair's gone pink," he said.

"Well, *your* hair's gone green!" said Farhan. Everyone stared.

Farhan's hair was pink. Oliver's hair was green. Claire's hair was blue, and Sima's hair was yellow!

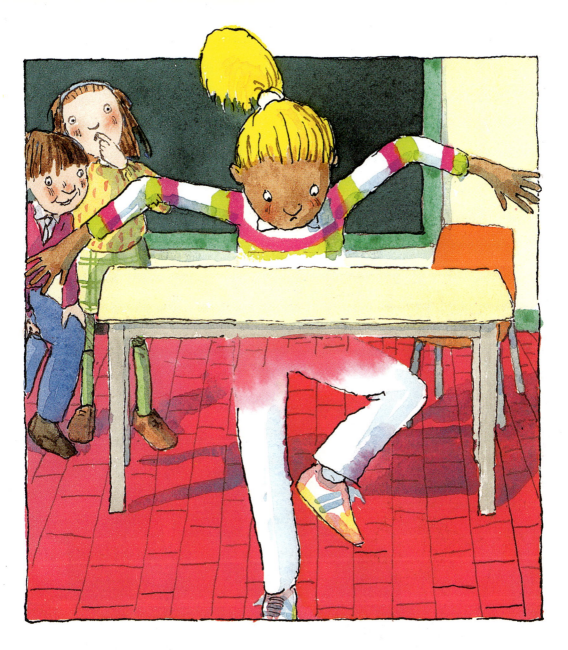

"Ugh!" yelled Sima. "Change it back!"

But, as she spoke, her legs began to disappear, then her body, then her arms, and then her head. "Help!" she shrieked.

At the same time, Oliver, Claire and Farhan disappeared. They were all invisible. "What's happening?" they yelled.

"Don't worry," said Mr Mulch to the rest of the class. "They're quite safe."

But the others didn't have time to worry about the four invisible children because Mr Mulch was already doing more amazing things. The posters on the wall were floating round the room like magic carpets and the waste-bin was hanging just below the ceiling.

Then all the chairs started to dance, jiggling about from one leg to the other. The children who were sitting on them leapt up immediately.

"Wow!" gasped Craig. "He really *is* nuts!"

Mr Mulch chuckled, and rubbed his hands together even faster.

"Come on, children," he shouted, "we'll make a pyramid!"
And before they knew what was happening, they found
themselves rising in the air and forming a perfect pyramid
with Mr Mulch at the top. Everyone was laughing and
shouting, while the posters and the waste-bin floated
round them.

Then the bell went for lunch. Mr Mulch clapped his hands and the children shot down to the floor. The chairs stopped dancing, and the posters and the waste-bin went back to their proper places.

"That was great!" said Sarah, smoothing down her hair.

Mr Mulch looked pleased. He pushed his spectacles back up to the top of his nose, picked up some books and went out.

"What about us?" yelled Oliver, Sima, Claire and Farhan. The rest of Class 8 looked round. The four children were still invisible.

Mr Mulch had forgotten them.

Sarah and Craig went to look for Mr Mulch, but they couldn't find him anywhere. They came back and joined the dinner queue.

"I'm hungry," wailed Claire. "I want my dinner."

"Me too," moaned Farhan.

But the invisible four didn't get anything. When they asked for their food, the dinner ladies got very cross. They thought the other children were copying the voices of Oliver, Sima, Claire and Farhan.

After lunch, Mr Mulch tried to make the four children visible again. He muttered and he rubbed his chin. He shut his eyes so that he could think better, but nothing seemed to work.

Then suddenly Claire's leg appeared. Mr Mulch smiled and let out a long sigh. "Aahhh!" he said.

Then Oliver's hand waved. "At last!" shouted Mr Mulch. "Hurrah," he gasped, when Farhan's tummy came into view. "There," he whispered, when Sima's head appeared.

But, whatever he did, he couldn't bring them back completely. He could only make bits of them reappear.

"Oh dear," he said at last, taking off his spectacles and cleaning them on the cuff of his jacket. "I'm afraid I must have forgotten the right magic."

There were shouts of rage from Oliver, Sima, Farhan and
Claire.

The rest of the class started to laugh. It looked so funny.
Claire's leg stamped on the floor, Oliver's hand flapped up and
down, Farhan's tummy breathed in and out and tears streamed
down Sima's angry face.

"Shh!" said Mr Mulch. "Be quiet. I have to concentrate."

"He can't send them home like that," whispered Sarah to Craig. "What will their parents say?"

"Perhaps he should rub a lamp, like they do at the pantomime," suggested Craig.

Mr Mulch stopped cleaning his spectacles and looked up. "What? What did you say, Craig?"

Craig looked embarrassed. "Er . . . I just said, perhaps you should rub something – a lamp or something. You know, like they do at the pantomime."

"BRILLIANT!" shouted Mr Mulch. His voice was so loud that everybody jumped. "Brilliant!" he repeated as he shoved his spectacles back on his nose and fumbled in the pockets of his jacket. "No, not here," he muttered. "Maybe it's in the trousers. Let me see now. I'm sure I still have one left."

Class 8 watched as Mr Mulch turned out all his pockets. He built up a heap of objects on the table in front of him. As these things came out, Mr Mulch looked sadder and sadder.

"I must have *one* left," he mumbled. "Surely there's *one* left!" He began to look really worried.

Frantically, he dug his hands into his pockets and turned the linings inside out. Suddenly, there was a clink as something flew out and dropped on the floor. "Ah!" shouted Mr Mulch as he scooped it up and held it between his finger and thumb.

Craig turned to Sarah. "It's only a coin," he said. He sounded disappointed.

Class 8 gathered round to look at it. At first they thought
it was an ordinary coin, but then they saw that it was covered
in strange symbols.

Slowly, Mr Mulch rubbed it backwards and forwards
between his hands. As he did so, the four invisible children
gradually reappeared. At last, Sima, Oliver, Claire and Farhan
were complete. Sima took a strand of her hair and carefully
checked its colour.

"What *is* that coin thing?" asked Sarah.

But Mr Mulch didn't answer.

Instead, he scooped up everything from the table, stuffed it back into his pockets and bounded towards the door.

"Goodbye, children!" he shouted. "I've got to go now."

Class 8 stared after him.

"He's amazing!" said Farhan.

"He's magic!" said Claire.

The next morning, Class 8 hurried into school. But there was a different teacher in the classroom – a new teacher.

"Where's Mr Mulch?" asked Sima, touching her hair nervously.

"Who?" said the new teacher.

"The man who came yesterday," said Oliver, looking round the classroom.

The new teacher narrowed her eyes.

"I don't know what you're talking about," she said.
"Now, settle down at once and get out your maths books."

Then, from beside the board, there came the sound
of someone laughing.

It was a familiar chuckle.

All the children turned to look. They couldn't see anyone,
BUT . . .